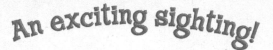

An exciting sighting!

Benjamin and Lucy walked off with Scott and Will, a short distance away from their parents. Benjamin knew that scientists had to be patient while waiting for their subjects to come along, but he could hardly wait to see a bear! He could see their giant paw prints in the mud, but no bears anywhere. He heard only birdcalls and the lapping of the water.

Then, suddenly, he saw something move about five hundred feet away. It just might be some blowing leaves, he thought. Or maybe a smaller animal, like a beaver. But when he caught sight of a distinctive face and fuzzy body, he knew at once that he was looking at a brown bear cub!

Books in the Jeff Corwin Series

JEFF CORWIN

JUNIOR EXPLORER SERIES: BOOK 2

THE GREAT ALASKA ADVENTURE!

Illustrations by Guy Francis

PUFFIN BOOKS
An Imprint of Penguin Group (USA) Inc.

To Natasha, Maya, and Marina

PUFFIN BOOKS
Published by the Penguin Group
Penguin Young Readers Group,
345 Hudson Street, New York, New York 10014, U.S.A.
Penguin Group (Canada), 90 Eglinton Avenue East, Suite 700, Toronto, Ontario,
Canada M4P 2Y3 (a division of Pearson Penguin Canada Inc.)
Penguin Books Ltd, 80 Strand, London WC2R 0RL, England
Penguin Ireland, 25 St Stephen's Green, Dublin 2, Ireland
(a division of Penguin Books Ltd)
Penguin Group (Australia), 250 Camberwell Road, Camberwell, Victoria 3124, Australia
(a division of Pearson Australia Group Pty Ltd)
Penguin Books India Pvt Ltd, 11 Community Centre,
Panchsheel Park, New Delhi - 110 017, India
Penguin Group (NZ), 67 Apollo Drive, Rosedale, North Shore 0632, New Zealand
(a division of Pearson New Zealand Ltd.)
Penguin Books (South Africa) (Pty) Ltd, 24 Sturdee Avenue,
Rosebank, Johannesburg 2196, South Africa

Registered Offices: Penguin Books Ltd, 80 Strand, London WC2R 0RL, England

Published by Puffin Books, a division of Penguin Young Readers Group, 2010

1 3 5 7 9 10 8 6 4 2
Copyright © Jeff Corwin, 2010
All rights reserved
Printed in the USA

LIBRARY OF CONGRESS CATALOGING-IN-PUBLICATION DATA IS AVAILABLE.

Puffin Books ISBN 978-0-14-241409-5

Printed in the United States of America

Dear Reader,

Before my family moved to a rural part of Massachusetts, we lived outside of Boston, where I wasn't always able to explore the natural world. So I had to find unique ways to discover the animals and plants around me—which led me right into my backyard! Even though I was living in a city, I found lots of amazing wildlife right outside my door. I just had to take a closer look!

And that's what the Baxter kids like to do in my Junior Explorer series—explore their immediate surroundings. Whether in the frozen wilderness or in their hometown near the Florida Everglades, Lucy and Benjamin Baxter always find ways to discover fascinating animals and plants. And so can you! It doesn't matter where you live—all you have to do is look outside, engage your curiosity about the natural world, and have fun discovering the plants, animals, and natural life around you.

Happy exploring!

Jeff Corwin

Chapter One

Nine-year-old Benjamin Baxter fumbled with his bike lock and groaned as he saw his younger sister, Lucy, pedal into the distance. She wasn't supposed to take off ahead of him—she was only eight, and the two of them were supposed to stick together after school. But that wasn't what was bothering him. What bugged him was that now she'd be the first one at their mom's office, and the first one there got dibs on the computer. Maybe Lucy would give him a turn, and maybe she wouldn't. Benjamin knew from experience that he shouldn't get his hopes up.

Click! The chain finally slid out of the lock. Benjamin wound it beneath his seat and took off after his sister. Two days a week, they biked to their mother's office after school. It was about half a mile away, on the top floor of the Life Sciences Building of the college where their mom taught biology. The office was cramped and filled with stacks of paper, but the Baxter kids loved having it to themselves while their mom finished teaching her classes.

Lucy liked to play games on the computer. That used to be Benjamin's favorite thing, too—until his mom showed him how to find the biology department's research files on the computer. Scientists from all over the world sent their data to the college, and with his mom's password, Benjamin could read their findings in the department database. He probably wouldn't get to look at them today, though. There was no way he'd get there before Lucy.

Benjamin tried not to think about everything he'd be missing today. He loved reading about what real live scientists were doing, and seeing how they shared their findings. But he didn't need a computer to learn more about the natural world, he reminded himself. It was all around him! Most people didn't see a college campus as an animal habitat, but Benjamin knew there were creatures in the freshly mown grass, the flower beds, even the eaves of the buildings.

There! He was biking past a row of shrubs, and he spotted a flash of bright green moving across the top. Benjamin stopped, reached out, and cupped it in his hand. It was a six-inch-long lizard called an anole. Anoles could change colors, like chameleons, and cling to walls, like geckos, but they were actually more closely related to iguanas. Benjamin took note of the small frill around the anole's neck, then sent it on its way before its skin developed the small dark spots that would indicate that it felt stressed. He'd describe the lizard in his notebook later.

It was strange to think that, in a few short days, he'd be in a place where no anole could survive on its own. The

Baxter family was about to take a
week-long trip to Alaska! One of his
mom's graduate students was working at a research station in Glacier Bay
National Park and, as her faculty advi-
sor, his mom had to see the student's
work firsthand. Alaska was far away,
and the kids would have to take a
whole week off from school, but their
parents had decided it was worthwhile
for the family to travel there together. A
"once-in-a-lifetime opportunity," their
parents had called it when they spoke

to their teachers. Benjamin and Lucy would each be taking assignments with them—they would each have to write a report, too—but they were willing to do the extra work. They were going to Alaska!

Benjamin was excited about every part of the trip—the places they'd see, the things he'd learn, even the report—but he wasn't too excited about the cold. It was only the middle of September, and it was already snowing in some parts of Alaska. Benjamin loved living in Florida—he never liked to wear more than a T-shirt and shorts if he could help it. So how would he tolerate the layers of clothes his mom said he would need? According to her, he needed long underwear, warm boots, thick socks, and even one of those ski masks that left only the eyes showing. He'd never seen anyone wearing one of those in Florida.

Coasting up to the Life Sciences Building, Benjamin locked his bike next to Lucy's in the rack. He took the elevator up and headed for his mom's office, where Lucy was sitting in front of the large-screen computer monitor. "Line up for a turn," she said as she turned over a seven of diamonds in her game. "First come, first served."

He knew better than to argue. "Fine by me," he said, shrugging. "I'll find something else to do." He filled his water bottle in a hallway fountain and lingered beneath a bulletin board where lectures and upcoming events were advertised. There was a poster for something called Semester at Sea—

that sounded pretty good to Benjamin. A visiting botanist was coming to the college to give a talk about houseplants. Another biologist was looking for a research assistant. All of this was a lot more interesting than playing cards on the computer, Benjamin thought. Especially for someone like him, who wanted to be a scientist when he grew up.

He heard footsteps in the stairwell. Could classes be over already? When the door opened, his mom was standing there with an oversize envelope. "Ben!" she said. "Have I got something to show you. You won't believe these pictures!" She headed into the office and opened the envelope. Inside were a dozen large photographs, which Beth Baxter spread across a long table. She stood with her hands on her hips, looking down at them in wonder.

Benjamin wasn't sure what he was seeing. It was a group of animals, some kind of whale, swimming together in a pod as thick as a school of fish. But even more strange, it looked like they had long horns extending from their mouths. "Swordfish?" he asked his mom, guessing.

"No! They're narwhals!" his mom exclaimed. (She always got really excited about animals.) "They're whales. They're in the same family as belugas, but male narwhals have these long tusks extending from their upper jaws." She pointed at the animals' horns. "Narwhals live in the waters off Greenland and northeastern Canada, where it can be hard to sail in the winter. These photos were taken from a plane."

Benjamin peered at the pictures. There had to be a hundred narwhals there, all heading the same way.

"What are they doing?" he asked.

"They're migrating," said his mom. "In the summer they stay in warmer, shallower water. But in the winter they go deep beneath the pack ice in the Arctic."

His mom sighed. "Take a good look at them. We might never see a pod like this again."

Benjamin looked up. "Why not?"

"Studies show that narwhals are especially vulnerable to climate change," his mom said. "They migrate along the same channels every year, and they eat only a narrow range of food. As their habitat changes, they'll have a hard time changing with it."

"How is their habitat changing?" Benjamin asked.

His mom explained. "Well, one effect of climate change is that the ice at the two poles is shrinking. And as it melts, the narwhals' territory is affected. They have less space under the ice for feeding. At the same time, with that smaller ice cover, other animals can reach places they couldn't reach before. So now killer whales, for instance, can get into the narwhals' territory to hunt them."

Thinking about ice reminded Benjamin of their upcoming trip. "Do narwhals live in Alaska?" he asked his mom.

"They don't," said Mrs. Baxter. "But we'll see plenty of other animals there, Ben. And some other evidence of climate change, too, I'm afraid."

Just then Lucy called to him from his mom's desk. "Benjamin!" she said. "Your turn!"

When the three of them arrived home that evening, there was a large box on their front porch. Benjamin could tell it was from a store that sold outdoor gear, and he didn't have a good feeling about it at all.

Sure enough, after dinner his mom made a big announcement. "Before I break out the ice cream," Beth Baxter said, "I need to make sure that your new coats fit. Consider the dessert an incentive," she said, looking right at Benjamin.

He put on his new down coat and gloves, his heavy boots, and his ski mask. He opened the package of long underwear only when everything else

was on already. "I'm stifling in this stuff," he said to his mom, his voice muffled by the mask. "Please can I try this on later, when I really need it?"

"Everything else seems to fit," his mom said. "I guess that's okay."

Suddenly Benjamin thought of something. "You know, Mom, winter's only starting in Alaska now—it can't be that cold yet."

"It will feel cold to you, I'm sure," she replied. "Trust me. It's better to be prepared."

Benjamin grinned. "But what about climate change?" he said. "Doesn't that mean it's getting warmer?"

Mrs. Baxter smiled and tossed a pair of wool socks at him. "Don't be fresh with me, young man, or I'll change the climate in this house!"

Chapter Two

In the bathroom at Juneau Airport, Benjamin wrestled into his gear. The Baxters had been traveling all day, and now it was nighttime in Alaska—four hours after night had arrived back home in Florida. Benjamin rubbed his eyes and waddled out of the bathroom stall. He was exhausted from the trip, and he could barely move in all his clothes. He waited for his father to come out of a stall, clomping in his boots, and the two returned to the baggage claim. They were ready to go out into the cold.

Mrs. Baxter and a sleepy-looking Lucy were talking to a tall man with a thick beard. "Will Jackson!" Mr. Baxter yelled, rushing to him. Benjamin exchanged a look with his sister. So this was their host for the first couple of nights in Alaska, before they left for Glacier Bay and, later, Nome. He was their parents' old friend from graduate school, and they hadn't seen him since he'd found a teaching job in Alaska, before Benjamin and Lucy were even born. Mr. Baxter exclaimed, "I'd know you anywhere!"

Will looked younger than their parents' other friends, Benjamin decided. He looked more like one of their students than one of their colleagues. Benjamin and Lucy had been disappointed to find out that, when they were with Will, there would be no other kids for them to hang out with. But now Benjamin was encouraged to see that Will looked like an overgrown kid himself, with his oversize jacket and his shaggy hair.

Will turned to the Baxter kids. "Glad to meet you two before you get into double digits! I've heard a lot about you!" He shook Lucy's hand, then Benjamin's. "So let me ask you this. You always dress so warmly?" His laugh boomed out across the airport, and Benjamin couldn't help grinning.

"I'd rather be in a T-shirt," Benjamin admitted. "I can't imagine having to dress like this all the time."

Will said, "Conditions can change on a dime here. You'll be glad you brought your gear. Tonight, though, you can probably get by in a warm sweater. Unless you listen to your parents." He winked at his old friends, guiding them out of the airport and into the Alaskan night.

By the time they got to Will's house, Benjamin was too tired to even notice where he was. But when he woke in the morning and went into the kitchen for breakfast, he checked out the view from the windows stretching around Will's kitchen table.

"It doesn't look like a city at all!" he told his mom, who was drinking her coffee. It looked more like a small town, with low-rise buildings and lots of trees.

"Did you know," she said, "you can't get here by car? You can only get to Juneau by plane, as we did, or by boat. And it's the state capital!"

Benjamin liked the sound of that—it made it seem so exciting. He also liked the way that tall mountains framed Will's house, and the way he could see water in the distance. He had never been in a city that felt so close to nature. Then Will walked into the kitchen and said something that really blew Benjamin's mind. "Welcome to the rain forest, Baxters!" Chuckling, he passed Benjamin a plate of muffins.

Benjamin wasn't sure he'd heard him right. They were thousands of miles from the tropics. "So . . . wait . . . how in the world can this be a rain forest?" he sputtered.

Will split his muffin in two. "Almost all of southeast Alaska is in the Tongass National Forest," he said. "One of the world's largest remaining temperate rain forests. People think of snow when they think of Alaska, but we get a lot of rain here, too. And all that moisture makes this a home for almost as many animals and plants as the tropical rain forests. Different species, and not nearly as diverse."

"I never knew there was any other kind of rain forest," Benjamin said.

"Temperate rain forests are located in temperate places," Will said. "Places where there are more people. Some of these forests have become centers of logging and other industry, just like in the tropical rain forests. But here the trees have grown to towering heights. You'll see," he said, reaching for the jam. "I thought that we'd take a drive out to Mendenhall Glacier today. You'll get a good sense of the terrain that way."

Lucy and their dad had come in as Will was talking. She smiled, a bit embarrassed, and asked, "Could you remind me what a glacier is again?" She knew she should know this, with two scientists for parents.

Mr. Baxter poured a cup of coffee and tried to explain. "It's a huge mass of ice, moving slowly," he said. He put one hand on top of the other and pressed on the table. "It's made out of snow that's fallen over many years and been compacted, like this. You find glaciers at the North Pole and South Pole and in most mountain ranges, but they're not usually as easy to see as they are here."

Benjamin was confused. "But how can there be a glacier in the rain forest?"

Will smiled. "The conditions are just right for it here—plenty of moisture, but never enough heat to thaw the ice all the way. Welcome to the wonderful world of Alaska!"

They couldn't have been more than ten minutes away from Will's house when suddenly Lucy was twisting around in the backseat of Will's car and digging her camera out of her pocket. She was staring at a tree they'd just driven by.

"Mom," she whispered, like she was trying not to disturb something. "Is that what I think it is?" She pointed to a bird that was perched on the tallest branch, looking out across the road toward the water on the other side, as if poised to dive in at any moment. Lucy's camera clicked rapidly.

It was a large bird with a black body, a yellow beak and talons, and a white head. Could it be a bald eagle? Benjamin thought. He'd read that recently they have been making a comeback; maybe it was.

In the front seat, Will nodded. "It is what you think it is. Bald eagles are all over the place here—in this part of Alaska alone, there's one for every three people. In fact, their population here has been growing so much that

they are no longer considered endangered. Our waters are extremely rich in fish and shellfish, a primary part of the bald eagle's diet. It's like an all-the-time, all-you-can-eat buffet for them."

Benjamin took out his notebook and drew a quick sketch of an eagle in it. (He and Lucy recorded their animal sightings in different ways.) They'd been in the state for less than twenty-four hours, and already it was full of surprises.

They drove up a winding road into the mountains, passing through woods so dense that Benjamin couldn't see past the row of trees by the side of the road. Then suddenly they were in a clearing with signs pointing to Mendenhall Lake. Will parked his car in a lot and led the Baxters up to the visitors' viewing center. "We're not going to be that close to the glacier," he said. "But from here you'll get the best sense of its size."

Benjamin was expecting it to seem small from a distance, like the buildings he'd seen from the top of the Empire State Building on his family's trip to New York. Instead, he drew his breath in sharply when he caught his first glimpse of it. The glacier was massive, like a mountain. It was covered in snow and mostly white, but its bottom was brown and green. The most startling thing was what was behind the glacier: an expanse of ice as far as he could see. "What's that?" he asked his dad. It looked just as he imagined the North Pole would.

"The Juneau ice field," his dad said. "Over thousands of years, snow and ice have accumulated there, never melting in the cool Alaskan summers. Gravity causes the ice to flow downhill slowly, away from the field. The glacier is the flowing ice. It's always moving toward the lake, where it ends. And along the way it scrapes the earth's bedrock, which is why it appears dirty on the bottom—it collects dirt and rocks as it goes!"

Lucy was looking longingly at the lake in front of the glacier. "I wish we could go out there," she said, pointing to some white shapes floating in the water. "Get a little closer, like those boats."

"Are you sure those are boats?" their dad asked mysteriously.

Benjamin stared at them for a moment, then cried, "Wait! I get it! They're icebergs!"

"You got it," Will confirmed. "Massive pieces of ice break off the glacier and fall into the lake. It's called calving. And trust me—you don't want to be anywhere near one of those things when they chip off! They can be as big as small buildings. That's why the visitors' center is way up here."

Benjamin stared out over the lake, taking in the view of the shining icebergs, with their weirdly irregular shapes. "It's amazing to think that the glaciers are constantly moving. I feel like we could watch them all day and not see a thing."

"Well, you'd need to do a bit more than stand around and watch to be able to detect the change," said Will. "But the process is speeding up as the earth warms overall. Actually, many scientists monitor climate change by watching what happens to the world's glaciers."

Climate change again, thought Benjamin. Change was a part of the natural world, he knew. Plants and animals, rocks and soil—they were always in flux, developing or dying. But the changing climate was bigger than all that.

Suddenly he had a great idea. He was supposed to be writing a five-page report about Alaska to hand in when he got back to school. His teacher had left the subject up to him, and he'd been worried about what part of Alaska to choose. An animal? A place? But if he wrote about climate change, he could include lots of different animals and places, as well as how they were all affected by global warming.

He and Lucy were always observing the natural world and recording what they saw. He recorded things in his journal—she took pictures. Maybe, on this trip, they could put their observations together to write a complete report about what Alaska was like before climate change changed anything else. He didn't see why they couldn't work together on one project—maybe ten pages instead of five—and turn it in to both of their teachers.

Benjamin made a mental note to mention it to his sister later. Now, though, he had an important mission to accomplish. He'd noticed there was a gift shop in the visitors' center. And he was pretty sure they had some awesome snow globes in Alaska!

Chapter Three

Shivering at a floatplane dock the next morning, Benjamin longed for Florida's hot sun. It wasn't long after dawn, and gray clouds threatened rain. The water was already dotted with fishing boats and ferries setting out for the day. The Baxters were waiting at the dock to fly from Juneau to Admiralty Island.

Will rubbed his hands together and

nudged Benjamin. "Brisk, isn't it?" he said.

Benjamin could see his breath in the air. It might not be a cold morning by Alaskan standards, but it was cold for him. And it wasn't even below freezing!

Inside the plane, though, he forgot all about the weather. He was too excited about where they were going:

Pack Creek, on Admiralty Island, to watch brown bears in the wild.

Will introduced the Baxters to his friend Scott, who'd be their guide for the day. "Scott has been flying folks out to Pack Creek for ten years now," he said. "He knows more about the bears than just about anyone."

"I was out there yesterday," Scott said, "and the bears were having a feast. This is the best time of year to see them—the salmon are still plentiful, but the summer crowds are gone. And before too long the bears will be gone for the winter, hibernating."

"We're ready!" said Lucy. She sounded as impatient as Benjamin felt.

The floatplane took off, soaring first over downtown Juneau and then setting out over the rest of the Tongass

National Forest. His mom was busy reading about bear safety, but Benjamin could only stare out the window. Below him was a landscape that looked as if no human had ever set foot in it. The mountains were heavily wooded, not crossed by any roads. And as the floatplane began to descend toward Admiralty Island, he could see one kayaker, paddling alone in the early morning. Benjamin wondered who it was, and what it felt like to be there. Probably like being one of the first explorers in Alaska, he thought. There were no towns, no cars, no stores on Admiralty Island, Scott told them. It was as wild as a place could be and still be easy to visit. If you had a floatplane, that is.

Benjamin could see his sister gripping

the arms of her seat, her knuckles turning white. "What's wrong?" he asked. He couldn't imagine why she was so upset.

"We're going down!" she said dramatically. Scott appeared to be flying toward the woods, where there was no open space to land a plane.

"I think floatplanes land in the water," he told Lucy. "That's why they're called floatplanes! It's also why they're big in Alaska—they can take people to wild places that don't have any landing strips."

Within minutes, Scott had coasted to a landing on the surface of the water. They were near solid ground, as Benjamin had expected, but not on it. He wasn't sure how they would get there till Scott opened up a box and started handing out rubber boots and rain gear. "The water's almost a foot deep," he said. "And cold, of course. But the gear will keep you warm and dry. Just follow me!" They waded through the water as he led them to a mudflat in front of thick forest. It looked like a wooded beach, with mud where there should have been sand.

Scott made sure they were all together. "This is the end of Pack Creek," he said, gesturing toward the mud. "The creek starts nearly four thousand feet up, in the mountains, and picks up sediment as it winds its way downhill. Here, that sediment creates a rich habitat for all kinds of shellfish, which brown bears love to eat. And even more important, this creek supports several runs of salmon."

Benjamin felt in the pocket of his jacket for his binoculars and put them around his neck. Scott noticed and said, "You don't have any food in there, do you?" Any snacks they'd brought were to be put in bear-proof boxes by the shoreline for safekeeping. "If you have food, the bears *will* get it," Scott assured the group. "They're wily creatures, intent on one thing: eating. They don't, however, have any interest in eating you. People have been coming to Pack Creek for decades to observe these bears, so they are used to being watched. We need to use common sense—don't approach them; don't make any loud noises. If we respect the bears, they will respect us."

The plan was to stay near the mudflat for a while, then take a mile-long hike up to an observation tower amid the trees. Benjamin and Lucy walked off with Scott and Will, a short distance away from their parents. Benjamin knew that scientists had to be patient while waiting for their subjects to come along, but he could hardly wait to see a bear! He could see their giant paw prints in the mud, but no bears anywhere. He heard only birdcalls and the lapping of the water.

Then, suddenly, he saw something move about five hundred feet away. It just might be some blowing leaves, he thought. Or maybe a smaller animal, like a beaver. But when he caught sight of a distinctive face and fuzzy body, he knew at once that he was look-ing at a brown bear cub! Its mother ambled behind it, looking carefully at the ground. She was as big as a small car, Benjamin estimated. Definitely the biggest animal he'd ever seen in person, outside a zoo.

"Lucy!" Benjamin said softly.

She looked in his direction, then grew wide-eyed as she noticed the bears. Slowly, so as not to startle them, she moved closer to her brother. "Do you think they saw you?" she asked.

"I'm not sure. They haven't looked at me, but I think they know I'm here." He could tell by the way they moved in every direction but toward him. "Maybe they smell me?" he mused.

"They probably hear us, too," Lucy said. "Even when we're whispering. Their hearing is really powerful."

Benjamin could hear Will and Scott walking behind them now.

He wondered how their footsteps sounded to the bears!

Benjamin watched the bears intently, hoping he'd remember everything to write down later. Lucy, meanwhile, was snapping pictures like crazy. The bears looked as cute and cuddly as stuffed animals, really. But then the mother reached into the mud and drew out a shell with her paw. Benjamin saw her long, sharp claws for a second, and caught a quick flash of her long teeth as she split the shell open and ate whatever was inside. The bears might look cute, but they were powerful predators, too.

The mother bear continued walking along, seeming to look for food. The cub suddenly made a dash for the water! Benjamin stepped away

instinctively, but the cub was nowhere near him or Lucy. It didn't seem to be looking for food or doing what its mother wanted. Instead, it caught a floating log and started to play with it! The cub tossed it in the water, swam after it, then tossed it again. Benjamin and Lucy watched quietly until the mother returned. She glanced at the cub, and it left the water immediately and followed its mother back into the woods. It was almost as if the cub knew it would get in trouble—just like when Benjamin's mother gave him "the look"!

The kids and Will and Scott joined Mr. and Mrs Baxter. "Amazing, aren't they?" Scott said, looking in the direction the bears had gone. "You guys want to see some more?"

They followed Scott up a narrow path through towering trees that blocked out the sky and the morning light. Eventually they came out into a small clearing with a wooden tower that reminded Benjamin of lifeguard stands he'd seen at the beach. "This is the island's bear observatory," Scott said. "The creek is right there, and the salmon are still spawning. I don't think we'll need to wait long for more bears."

Benjamin nodded as if he understood what Scott meant, but he didn't fool his mom. "Pacific salmon hatch and live the first part of their lives in freshwater rivers and streams like this one," Mrs. Baxter explained. "Then they swim out to the ocean. Their time in the ocean can range from six months to seven years, depending on the species, but when they're ready to lay their eggs, they swim back to the exact same river or stream where they were born. Once they lay their eggs, the journey of the adult salmon ends. But after they die, they still give back to the Earth, becoming food for a bald eagle or a bear, or nourishing the soil so plants can grow. And their eggs hatch in the stream, and the young salmon swim back to the ocean to repeat the cycle."

"So it's one big cycle of life," Mr. Baxter chimed in.

"So the salmon are coming back right now?" Benjamin asked. It was weird to think that the salmon were migrating *to* Alaskan streams just as other species would be migrating *from* Alaska for warmer places, clearing out of the area for the winter.

Scott said, "Pack Creek is so full of salmon now that the water is thick with them. There are hundreds of fish in any short stretch."

"Hang on a second," Mr. Baxter said. His specialty was ecology, the way that different species depend on and interact with one another and their environments. "You're leaving out all the drama! What's most amazing about salmon migration is that it

happens at all, considering the odds. Out at sea, salmon are threatened by fishing nets, not to mention larger fish. They can be extremely far from the place of their birth. And even if they make it back to their original stream—exhausted and hungry—they face another set of predators before they can lay their eggs."

"Like brown bears?" Benjamin asked. It looked like some salmon might be running out on their luck just now.

As his father spoke, a pair of adult bears had approached the creek. His mother whispered just loud enough to be heard. "The bears know this is spawning season," she said. "And they will be hibernating soon, so they need to eat all they can for the winter. To get here, the salmon have had to be strong and resilient. But even a tough fish is no match for a hungry bear."

The Baxters' group watched as more bears emerged from the woods. Some perched on the side of the water, some waded in—and all scooped up big pawfuls of fish from the stream! The Baxters and their friends watched the bears gorge themselves on the salmon, then they hiked back to the plane to open the backpacks that carried their lunches.

On the narrow path, Benjamin stopped for a moment to take a quick drink from his water bottle. In the second that his face was tilted upward, he spotted another bald eagle soaring overhead, plus a V-shaped group of Canada geese flying south. Benjamin smiled to himself—if there were any more wildlife up there, Admiralty Island would need its own air traffic controller!

Chapter Four

In his excitement over the bears, Benjamin had forgotten all about suggesting a joint project to Lucy. That night in Juneau, though, his father lent them his laptop, and the Baxter kids started working on some of their school assignments. After a few pages of math homework, Benjamin was ready to think about something else. That's when he proposed his climate-change project to Lucy: a ten-page report, for both of their teachers, in which they described Alaska as it was right now, in both words and pictures. His parents thought that was a great idea, and Will said they could borrow his printer. Lucy had a lot of questions, but when she heard that Will had said they could borrow his printer, she started printing out photos right away.

"It won't be just kid stuff," Benjamin said importantly, taping the pictures into his notebook. "Like what people usually bring back from family trips. This could be a record for real scientists to use. Someday someone will want to know what Alaska was like *today*. If they see and read our findings, scientists can compare them to their findings in the future and figure out what's changed."

"It's kind of a big subject," Lucy said. "Alaska is the largest of the fifty states, and we're only visiting a few places."

"I know," replied Benjamin. "My idea is that we record as much as we can about what we see. Our teachers will be interested because it's about our trip. But it could be important to other readers, too."

Lucy looked at him curiously. "How will anybody else find out about our report?" she asked.

"I haven't really worked out that part . . . ," Benjamin admitted.

Real scientists might not be reading their work quite yet. But the kids would be visiting with real scientists on the next part of their trip. Before they explored Glacier Bay National Park, Mrs. Baxter needed to check in with her student, Hope, who was studying wolves in the park. After Mrs. Baxter had confirmed that they'd all be safe, she'd invited the whole family to join her.

Will decided to come along, too. "I've known your parents since their very first classes in grad school," he said. "Back then, we didn't know they'd become such experts in their fields." Will winked at Mr. Baxter and said, "At times, it seemed like your dad might only become an expert on eating pizza and watching football on TV!"

Part of Benjamin wanted to hear more stories about his parents before they had kids, but Will had already moved on to telling them about the park. They followed him out of the Glacier Bay Lodge, where they'd left their belongings in a small cabin, and headed toward a dock. Mrs. Baxter's student would be meeting them with a boat to take them out to her research station.

"Here's what you need to know," Will said. "Two hundred years ago, this park was covered by a glacier. Since then, the glacier has retreated nearly sixty-five miles, exposing open water and earth where nothing had grown for thousands of years. The environment here is changing every day."

"But it's not climate change, exactly, is it?" Lucy asked, looking at her brother.

"Climate change may change the

way it happens here," Will explained. "But, no, this movement is part of the natural life of glaciers."

Mr. Baxter took it from there. "One way to think of it is that glaciers wipe the earth's slate clean. Nothing grows when the earth is covered in ice; but as the ice moves, plants crop up first, then animals begin to move in."

Mrs. Baxter pointed to a forested area near the water. "Here, where the glacier has been gone for many years, you can see mature trees. As you travel farther inland, the trees are smaller and younger, until you get to an area where the glacier has permanently melted or moved out and new growth is beginning."

"So where do the wolves come in?" Benjamin asked.

His mom made it all sound so simple. "As the new forests grow, animals see new habitats and new places to feed. The smaller ones come first, and the larger ones follow. The first moose were spotted in the park the year I was born. Now the park is full of other large animals, too, like brown bears and wolves—the natural predators of moose. Hope and her team are trying to identify the number of wolves."

"And what have they found?" Benjamin asked eagerly.

"Let's go and see!" his mom said with a smile, waving to a young woman in a boat. "There's Hope now."

The research station was not quite as grand as it sounded. It was basically just a few tents in the wilderness, where Mrs. Baxter's student and some others had been camping out for several weeks. With winter approaching, though, the team was ready to wrap up its project.

Hope was a student whom Benjamin remembered from Florida. She'd worked with his mom before, so she knew the Baxter kids, but at first she was so busy with the adults that she barely said hello to Benjamin and Lucy. When the adults settled in to look at some data, though, Hope took the kids aside. "Do you guys want to hear something cool?" she asked.

Without explaining, she led the kids into one of the tents, where a sleek black box sat on a makeshift table. It was squawking intermittently—it sounded almost like Morse code—but

Benjamin had no clue what he was listening to.

He looked at his sister, who shrugged. "Whale songs?" she guessed.

"More like wolf songs," said Hope. "We've managed to put radio collars on a number of wolves since we've been out here," she explained. "Those are the radio signals they're transmitting back to us. These sounds tell us about the size of their packs, where their dens are, and where they go to look for prey." She showed them a map where the team had been pinpointing the locations of the signals all over the woods and mountains. "One pack seems to be living around here," she said. "And another has a den over here. We think there are about twenty-five wolves in each pack."

Hope showed them some photos and videos her group had taken. "When we put it all together, we get a broad picture of how wolves are living in the park right now. Your mom will be sending researchers here next year, too, and the year after that, so they can compare the data and see how the population is growing."

"See?" said Benjamin, nudging his

sister. "Her report is like our report—a snapshot in time."

Lucy ignored him. "Do you think we'll see a wolf today?" she asked.

"Not up close," said Hope. "Like most wild animals, they tend to steer clear of people. But keep an eye out while you're in the park. You can often spot where they've been, because you can see what they've been eating. And, of course, you can hear them, since they howl to communicate with other members of their pack."

Benjamin thought about his dog, Daisy, back home. She would be terrified of coming too close to a wolf, he knew. And he would probably be a little afraid, too, though he might not want to say it out loud. But wouldn't it be awesome to catch a glimpse of one? Benjamin vowed to keep an eye out for wolves during the rest of their time in the park. The only problem was that they were getting on board a tour boat next, and if there was one place he wasn't likely to see a wolf, it was the water.

The boat tour wasn't for the faint of heart. Dark clouds had blown in over Glacier Bay National Park, and the choppy water was making people feel sick. Benjamin and Lucy, though, stood on the deck with their binoculars while the grown-ups watched from inside, where it was warmer. Other passengers wandered in and out, but the Baxter kids mostly had the deck to themselves.

Benjamin zoomed in on a small

beach, scanning it for signs of more bears, or moose. He knew the beach was teeming with life, even if it looked deserted to the human eye; and where there were fish and shellfish there would be other animals to eat them. A couple of sleek, black-and-white loons bobbed near the shore, and familiar-looking seagulls were patrolling the sky, ready to swoop in when a good meal washed up on the rocks. Benjamin recorded everything he noticed in his notebook, making quick sketches of the birds as they passed by. Observe and record . . . that was what science was all about, he knew.

Suddenly Lucy nudged him. "Look!" she said, putting her binoculars down for a moment and pointing. In the water beside the boat, several sea otters were swimming! They had furry faces, and the kids could see their long webbed feet as they moved along. "Did you know that sea otters are in the same family as skunks and weasels?" Lucy asked Benjamin. He didn't know that, actually. "They can weigh up to seventy pounds," Lucy said. "They can walk on land, but they are capable of living exclusively in water."

Benjamin was always amazed at how his sister had all these facts at her fingertips, but then again, she loved learning about animals. In a moment, a park ranger's voice came over a loudspeaker to share some more information with the tour group. "Sea otters have the most dense fur of any other creature on Earth! They can dive deep under water for food and use tools, like rocks and shells, to open prey like urchins and snails, which they love to eat." He also said the number of sea otters in Alaska was dropping dramatically, partly because they were vulnerable to oil spills, but also partly due to changes in patterns of orca feeding. As the tour boat sailed farther up the Y-shaped bay, Benjamin could begin to see evidence of the different growth stages that his father had been talking about. Up ahead, the spruce trees looked shorter, the woods less dense. And it was all because this part of the park was still coming to life. It was a lot to keep straight, actually. Ecosystems were constantly changing and evolving. Then, on top of all that, the climate was changing, too, and every species was forced to adapt.

His thoughts were interrupted by an unusual barking sound. He turned to his right and noticed that the boat was approaching a rocky island. The sound seemed to be coming from the island, but Benjamin couldn't quite figure it out until he noticed the rocks were moving. They weren't rocks at all— they were sea lions! "Lucy!" he said. But she was already snapping pictures with her camera.

On the loudspeaker, the ranger explained that these were Steller sea lions, the largest type of sea lion and native to the northern Pacific. "And you may be wondering what the difference is between a sea lion and a seal," the ranger continued. "Well, seals have short, fur-covered front flippers with claws. And they roll around to move rather than walk, like sea lions do. But right now, these sea lions don't seem to want to walk anywhere." He laughed as Ben and Lucy looked again at the sea lions. They were basking on the rocks, resting between meals. They didn't really seem to be resting, though, so much as jostling for the best spots on the rocks. The barking was the sound they made as they tried to muscle one another out of the way! They were large animals with bulging eyes and light brown skin. It was hard to see from a distance, but Benjamin thought he saw hair around some of their faces, almost like manes. Sure enough, the ranger said, "These creatures were named by a German naturalist, Wilhelm Steller, who described them as 'lions of the sea.' Not only

do they bear a passing resemblance to lions—they sound like lions, too!"

As the boat passed the island, Benjamin could see water shooting up into the air in the distance. He and Lucy exchanged a glance. Was this what they were waiting for?

The ranger's voice came over the loudspeaker again, sounding excited. "Ahead of us is a pod of humpback whales," he said, "coming up for air! What looks like water shooting up is really the vapor they exhale through their blowholes before diving down to look for more food."

Benjamin stood at the railing in awe as the blowing stopped and suddenly two magnificent black-and-white tails, called flukes, emerged from the water. "When the whales are ready to dive, their tails are often visible," the ranger said. "And when they come to the surface to rest between dives, they blow as often as every few seconds. That'll make it easy for us to follow them."

The tour boat stayed with the whales for almost half an hour—and the whales stayed with the tour boat, too. They swam beneath the boat and popped up on the other side, all while the ranger told the group more about them. "Humpbacks are baleen whales," he said, "meaning that they don't have teeth, but rather a comb-like filter made of material similar to hair—called the baleen—that allows them to take in small fish while keeping out other animals. And they eat a lot! These whales eat up to one and a half tons of food a day and can weigh up to forty tons! And they are finishing up their year's feast right about now," he added, "before they begin their long migration south. Humpbacks from this part of Alaska spend their winter in the waters off Hawaii. They won't eat while they're there, though. Instead, they'll survive on the fat they've stored up during the summer months."

Benjamin was feeling grateful that they were here in September. It was starting to sound as if all the interesting animals would be asleep or away for most of the winter!

Suddenly, a humpback made a big splash to his left. As Benjamin watched,

it launched itself entirely out of the water, twisted around, and crashed back in. The whale was bigger than a school bus, and its skin glistened in the afternoon light.

It was only visible for a few seconds, but the memory of it stayed in Benjamin's mind long after the tour boat had moved away. He had never seen such a magnificent creature—and wished so much to see more of it! He still liked the idea of his report for school, capturing a moment in time in Alaska. But this was a moment he wished he could relive again and again.

Chapter Five

The Baxters got back to the lodge about an hour before dinner. The grown-ups wanted to rest, but Benjamin could think of nothing but working on his report. With his notebook open on the bed beside him, Benjamin typed up his notes on his dad's laptop. Then Lucy connected her camera and downloaded photos into the text. They had four pages already! "Looks good!" Lucy said, almost surprised. Then both kids spent half an hour reading before they ate.

In the morning, they would be leaving for Nome, a remote town on the Bering Sea that their parents wanted to visit while they were in Alaska. Before bed, Benjamin took out a guidebook to learn a little bit about it. Nome, it turned out, was way on the other side of the state, and much farther north. It definitely wasn't the rain forest! Benjamin had loved his time in southeast Alaska, but he was also curious about seeing the kind of Arctic landscape he'd imagined before they left Florida. "Look!" he said to Lucy, showing her a map. "Nome is just one hundred and two miles south of the Arctic Circle. And only one hundred and thirty-one miles east of Russia!"

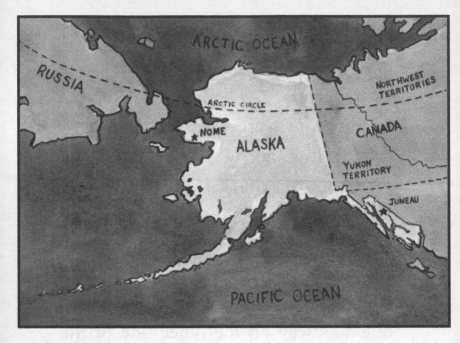

When their bags were packed the next morning, their parents led them quietly down the hall. It was still early, and they didn't want to wake the other guests—especially Will, who was heading back to Juneau later that day. But Benjamin could see Will waiting at the door. He was totally confused . . . until he saw that Will's bag was packed, too.

"I've been thinking," Will said,

"about saying good-bye to you Baxters for another ten years. And I'm not quite ready to do it yet. I go to Nome a few times a year, so I know the ropes. I thought I'd check in on my colleague out there, who's part of a group of us studying coastal erosion. Of course, I can also show you around!"

And it was that easy! From the lodge, Will made the necessary arrangements, and he boarded the plane with the Baxters to Nome. Benjamin was happy to have him along, and enjoyed seeing how eager Will was to share information and findings with his fellow scientists.

As soon as they landed, Benjamin could see what set Nome apart from the Juneau area. He didn't see any trees! His mother noticed it, too, and said, "Trees can't grow here because they can't put down roots in the permanently frozen soil, called permafrost. Towns are also affected by this permafrost. In fact, because the permafrost is melting, buildings and houses are sinking into the ground. And some people have had to move."

Ben looked at his mom, almost in disbelief. "It doesn't rain very much, either," she continued. "So only low-growing plants like shrubs and mosses can really thrive." Benjamin could feel that it was much colder now that they were farther north—definitely below freezing—and there was a dusting of snow on the ground. He was glad he had his cold-weather gear.

If Juneau, Alaska's capital, had felt

like a small town, well, Benjamin hadn't seen what a really small town looked like. Nome had no more than four thousand people, hardly any traffic, and only three roads out of town— many of which came to a stop in the middle of nowhere, Will told them. The first thing they did when they left the airport was take a drive down one of these roads, just to see the spectacular scenery. Two minutes after they left Nome behind, the Baxters and Will were in the only car on a gravel road heading into a vast open space. It was like a cold prairie, covered in grasses and with seemingly no limit to the sky.

Will said, "Nome was one of Alaska's gold-rush towns. Its population swelled to ten times what it is now, and mining towns sprang up in the wilderness. A railroad was quickly built to transport gold from the remote towns, but the tracks were washed away in a storm, and these trains were stranded."

As they came around a turn in the road, Benjamin could see a handful of rusted steam locomotives, looking like they had chug-chugged right out of an old movie. They were a strange, haunting sight in the middle of the desolate landscape—and even stranger in contrast to the herd of animals that stood behind them!

"Reindeer!" Lucy cried.

"Caribou!" said Benjamin.

"Actually, they're both," Will explained. "The same animal is called reindeer in Europe and caribou in America. There are more caribou than

people in Alaska! They're one of the largest members of the deer family, and they're unusual because both the males and the females grow antlers."

The large herd was moving through an area of scrubby shrubs. Benjamin couldn't begin to count them— it would be an impressively large number—so instead he focused his binoculars on one at a time. "Check out their hooves," his dad said, beside him. "See how they're wide at the bottom? They've adapted so caribou can roam the tundra both in the summer, when the top layer is soft and spongy, and in the winter, when it is frozen. In the snow, those large hooves act almost like snowshoes! Plus the caribou can also use them as paddles for swimming—and for running almost as fast as our car is going right now."

Benjamin couldn't quite imagine one piece of equipment that could do all those things for him. It would be like wearing snowshoes, beach shoes, running shoes, and flippers all at once!

Lucy, meanwhile, was looking in the other direction. "What are those?" she asked cautiously. Benjamin whirled around in the backseat to see another herd of animals, on the other side of the road, looking as if they'd stepped right out of the Ice Age. They had cowlike faces, but their bodies were covered in long fur and horns that began at the top of their heads, grew down, and curved up at the end. They moved slowly as they grazed on the dry grasses.

"Those are musk ox," Will told them. "They've wandered this part of the world since the time of the woolly

mammoth. He described the unusual way the musk ox defended themselves against predators, drawing in a tight circle around their calves when a wolf or a bear approached. But what struck Benjamin most was how ancient a species they were. It was amazing to think that, back when they'd roamed with the mammoths ten thousand years ago, this landscape hadn't looked much different from what it did now, except that now the permafrost was melting because of climate warming.

On the way back into town, Will talked a little bit about how the tundra has been changing. He told them that with shorter, warmer winters, the layers of frozen earth beneath the tundra could thaw, creating an unstable environment for the animals that lived there. The permafrost, as it was called, would also release large amounts of carbon into the air as it thawed. Carbon was one of the gases causing climate change in the first place, and widespread release of large amounts would speed the process.

When they arrived at the small hotel where they would be staying, Will invited the kids for a walk on Nome's beach. "No work," he said, "just play. Actually . . . it's the perfect place to fly a kite, and I know just where we can find one." He led them to a local store. Benjamin couldn't take his eyes off all the unique crafts for sale there. He would make sure he went back there with his parents, since he really wanted to find something special to bring home from their trip. He'd collected magnets and a snow globe back in Juneau, but he was still looking for a memento he couldn't find anyplace else.

The kites were hanging on a wall near the door, and Benjamin and Lucy looked at them while Will spoke to the clerk. The kids could see the colors of the kites, but not the shapes. "I think this one is a regular one," Lucy said, holding out a package wrapped in plastic. "But this one is some kind of animal . . . I can't tell what."

Suddenly a boy was next to them, checking it out. "That one's a penguin," he said, glancing at the package.

"A penguin?" Benjamin said, surprised. "But penguins don't really fly . . . isn't that a strange design for a kite?"

The boy grinned at him. "Yeah. Plus there are no penguins here in Alaska! You wouldn't believe how many people come here looking for penguins," he told them.

The Baxter kids picked a plain red kite instead, and the boy gave them directions to the best place to fly it. "When you get to the beach, walk to your left," he said. "If anyone asks, say Eli sent you!"

Benjamin was pretty sure he was kidding—there was nobody to tell! Nome's beach was deserted, and Benjamin could see why. The air was cold, yes, but the real problem was the wind, whipping frigid air around his face and ears. He found the ski mask his mom had bought him stuffed in the pocket of his parka, so he put it on. It made him look ridiculous, he was sure, but he was glad to have it. Ahead of him on the sand, Lucy pulled up her hood and wrapped her wool scarf over her face.

In spite of the cold, though, Benjamin thought the beach was beautiful. Back home in Florida, the beaches were never empty, and it was hard to notice their natural beauty when there were so many people around. Here, though, there was nothing to distract from the rhythm of the water or the stretch of the horizon. Benjamin imagined that not so far away, there were kids standing on a Russian beach, facing Nome.

Will got the kite up, and the Baxter

kids ran along the beach with him as he reeled it out. "This beach is where the first prospectors found gold in Nome," Will said. "People say there are still flakes of gold in the sand. And occasionally you'll see a polar bear out here, too."

Lucy's eyes widened under her scarf. "Any chance we'll see one today?" she asked breathlessly.

Will shook his head. "Probably not," he said. "They live on sea ice, or frozen ocean water, which is just beginning to build up in Nome in September. Right now, most polar bears are north of here, where the sea ice has already accumulated for this winter—or never melted from years past."

"But if we came back in January, they might be here?" Lucy asked.

"I think that's a good bet," Will said, smiling.

Benjamin wondered when, if ever, he would be back. He would love to see a polar bear up close, the way he'd seen the brown bears on Admiralty Island. But a real scientist would make the most of what he could see, he told himself. A real scientist would observe the ice and record the conditions in Nome before the bears returned. Nothing was happening on the beach here—nobody was around to distract him, except Will and Lucy with the kite. So he sat down, found a big rock to hold down the flapping pages of his notebook, and started to write right there, in the wind, describing everything he could see.

Chapter Six

Benjamin woke up, blinking, in the Nome hotel the next morning. It was still early, he could see from his watch, but the light in the room was bright. As if the sun had been up for hours, or as if . . .

He sprang out of bed and walked to the window, wondering. And it was true! It had snowed during the night! Benjamin stood still for a few minutes, looking at the way the clean snow blanketed the street, the roofs, everything. It couldn't be more than a few inches, he estimated, but he'd never seen so much snow in his life, except in movies. It was amazing! He sketched a quick picture in his notebook and woke up Lucy, too. She said, "Now it looks like Alaska should," and Benjamin totally agreed.

When the Baxters met Will for breakfast in the small dining room downstairs, he was holding a brochure. "I was worried we'd have to leave Nome without a dogsled ride," he said, smiling. "But the snow makes

this a perfect day to get out there!"
Local mushers—dogsled drivers—
catered to visitors, and Will quickly
arranged for them to have a ride.

The dogsled was waiting for them
on the outskirts of town, where snow-
plows were still scraping snow off the
roads. Not that they would be going on
the roads, Benjamin realized. Dogsleds
allowed travelers to get between places
that didn't have paved roads. People
had been crossing the Alaskan wilderness on dogsleds for hundreds of years.

The musher was harnessing eight
dogs, in teams of two, up and down

a long line. They were all Siberian huskies, with piercing blue eyes and wolflike markings on their fur. (Actually, a couple of the dogs had one blue eye and one brown eye, which Benjamin knew was a common trait in huskies.) They barked and squirmed a little as they were clipped in, but they were clearly ready to do their job. The basket of the sled was suspended a few inches above the snow, with runners sticking out behind it. The musher would stand on the runners to drive the sled. Benjamin climbed into the basket, and suddenly they were off!

"Pretend you're in the Iditarod!" Benjamin said into the wind as the dogs started running. He and Lucy were sharing one sled, while the adults were on another sled just behind them.

"The what?" asked his sister.

"The Iditarod!" Benjamin yelled. "The famous dogsled race!" The dogs were picking up speed and it was hard to talk. "A hundred years ago, there was an outbreak of diphtheria here in Nome, and no way to get medicine to the sick people, since there was so much snow. Then somebody put together a dogsled relay, where one dog team would take the medicine as far as one town, then another team would pick it up, and on and on."

"So it got here eventually?" Lucy asked, concerned.

Benjamin nodded. "Yeah, the dog-sleds saved the whole town! And now there's a dogsled race every winter along the same one thousand, one hundred and fifty-mile route, in memory of the dogs and mushers who were part of the relay. It starts near Anchorage and ends here in Nome. And it's a tough race. Teams brave below-zero temperatures and freezing cold winds. It takes about two weeks to finish, but one team finished in a record nine days! It's one of Alaska's biggest tourist attractions."

They were well out of Nome now, in a winter wonderland. The distant mountains were capped with snow, and where they'd seen grass and shrubs the day before, there was only white.

A lone moose wandered nearby, unbothered by the rushing dogs. Lucy snapped more pictures, while

Benjamin just tried to take it all in. This was everything he had expected of Alaska, and more. In this moment, so far from human activity, it seemed like nothing could ever change except maybe the season and the time of day.

When the ride was finished and they climbed out of the sleds, Mrs. Baxter said what Benjamin was thinking. "Can't get much more Alaskan than that."

Will had another surprise waiting for them. "I know it's cold out, and this is the last thing on your mind. But are you guys up for some ice cream? Alaskans love the stuff—they eat more of it than people in any other state." To Benjamin's surprise, he led them into the same store where they'd bought the kite. "You can get just about anything here," Will said. "Their ice cream is the best-kept secret in town."

Their parents placed the family's order at a small cooler in the back, while Benjamin and Lucy roamed through the aisles they'd missed the day before. There were groceries in one row, hardware in another, and warm socks and gloves in the one after that.

"I wonder if they have postcards?" Lucy said, keeping an eye out for souvenirs.

"You have enough pictures already," Benjamin teased. "But take a look at these!" He was standing at the counter of crafts he'd seen before. There were some cool masks and baskets, but what really drew his eye were some small white carvings. "Look, Lucy! Dogs and a dogsled!"

Then Eli—the boy with the kites—appeared on the other side of the counter and said, "Can I help you?" That's when Benjamin realized why he knew so much about the kites: he worked here! Benjamin was startled to see a kid his age helping out in the store, but there was an adult working the register—probably one of his parents, Benjamin guessed. "Can you tell me about these?" he asked, pointing to the dogs.

The boy smiled. "My mother carved them, actually. They're made out of ivory from walrus tusks," explained the boy. "It's a traditional Inupiaq handicraft." He picked up some other carvings for them to see: tiny boats and caribou, an intricate knife handle. Benjamin wondered how long they took to carve, but he didn't want to be too nosy.

Instead, he asked, "Where do the walrus live?" He would love to see one before they left.

The boy sighed. "They live on the sea ice," he said. "But it doesn't last as long here as it used to. The changing climate is forcing animals—and people—to change their habits."

Benjamin knew that animals had to adapt as the earth warmed. It was a challenge for Arctic animals like polar bears. But people had to adapt, too—he'd never really thought about that. And it seemed as if Lucy hadn't, either, because suddenly she wanted to know more.

"Are things different for you?" she asked curiously.

The boy rearranged the items in the display. "Well, my family moved into town because of the melting perma-frost. And my dad and I used to go hiking all the time, but now we only go every now and then. The melting per-mafrost has really changed our lives."

Lucy nodded. "So . . . what do you do for fun here in town?" she asked. "I mean, besides flying kites on the beach?"

Eli shrugged. "Probably what you do at home . . ." he trailed off.

"We live in Florida!" Lucy cried.

"Okay, so maybe not," said Eli. "Have you ever ridden a snowmobile?"

"We've never even made a snow-man!" Benjamin admitted.

"I don't really do much of that stuff, anyway," Eli said. "When I'm not in the store, I like to hike in the tundra and the mountains, collecting plants

and rocks. I want to be a scientist when I grow up!"

Benjamin and Lucy looked at each other. "So do we!" said Lucy.

"Maybe . . . we could work on something together," Benjamin suggested shyly. "We're doing a report for school, and maybe you could help share some information with us. . . ."

Since they were so far north, the sun set long before they finished dinner that night. In the morning, the

Baxters would board a plane back to Glacier Bay, while Will would meet with his colleagues in Nome. The kids took turns thanking him before they went to bed. "I feel like we've really gotten to know Alaska," Benjamin said. "So much more than we could have on our own. Thank you!"

Will promised to keep in touch. He would send periodic updates from Alaska, he promised, with descriptions and photos the kids could compare to those they'd collected firsthand.

But Will wouldn't be Benjamin's only source of information now. Eli would be in touch, too. He promised to send Benjamin a report of when the sea ice stretched down to Nome, when he sighted his first polar bear of the season, and when the Inupiaq walrus hunt began. Then they could measure their results against past and future years, getting a real sense of how climate change was changing things right here. Mr. Baxter had given Benjamin permission to share his e-mail address, so he could communicate with Eli easily.

Benjamin realized that this wasn't all that different from the way Will and his fellow researchers shared their information. Or how Hope and his mother worked together. Maybe I'll be a real scientist sooner than I think—capturing not just one moment in Alaska, but the way things are evolving here, Benjamin thought before he went to sleep.

He couldn't wait to tell everyone at school about what he'd seen in Alaska—and what he would continue to learn.

Meet the Baxters as they explore
Brooklyn in Book 1 of the
JUNIOR EXPLORER SERIES.

And read more of the Baxter kids'
adventures in the next book in the series!